THE OBERON BOOK OF
COMIC MONOLOGUES FOR WOMEN

KATY WIX

The Oberon Book of

COMIC MONOLOGUES

FOR WOMEN

Foreword by
Jennifer Saunders

OBERON BOOKS
LONDON

WWW.OBERONBOOKS.COM

First published in 2014 by Oberon Books Ltd
521 Caledonian Road, London N7 9RH
Tel: +44 (0) 20 7607 3637 / Fax: +44 (0) 20 7607 3629
e-mail: info@oberonbooks.com
www.oberonbooks.com

A catalogue record for this book is available from the British
Library.

PB ISBN: 978-1-84943-428-7
E ISBN: 978-1-84943-942-8

Cover design by James Illman

Printed, bound and converted
by CPI Group (UK) Ltd, Croydon, CR0 4YY.

Acknowledgements

Many thanks to Andrew and everyone at Oberon Books. A big thank you to Alice Russell, Rob Aslett and Lily Williams. A special thank you to Jennifer Saunders and thank you very much Mandy Wix. Much gratitude to Clara Brennan, Anna Starkey, Marianne Buckland, Anna Crilly, Sophie Black and Henry Petrides.

Contents

FOREWORD

So Katy Wix has written this book of comic monologues and I may have to steal some of them. Although written for the female voice, I dare say they would stand up very well if you were a gentleman and changed the odd word or two. Here you have a book filled with brilliant characters and much funny. Each piece is bubbling with the quirky genius that makes Miss Wix one of the funniest performers / writers around.

If I was ever called to audition, which I am not often despite being largely available and willing to try my hand at most things, I would be most grateful to Miss Wix for this fantastic collection. However most likely I shall keep it by my bed to dip into for laughs.

It is a very good read.

Well done Miss Wix.

Jennifer Saunders
March 2014

INTRODUCTION

Hello.

Thanks for buying this book! I hope you enjoy my first collection of humorous monologues for women. I have written forty original comedic speeches intended for performance, which you will hopefully enjoy reading, even if you're not a performer yourself. The monologues are designed for actresses of all ages, accents, backgrounds, heights and star-signs.

During my time at drama school, I remember struggling to find a modern, funny audition speech that I really engaged with and that hadn't been heard numerous times before so I began writing my own monologues for myself and the other students, which is how this anthology came into fruition.

Dramatic monologues are a very effective way of capturing the ebb and flow of thoughts and feelings that pass through a character. The directness of the monologue can create a brief moment of intimacy with an audience, which can have much impact, creating the perfect blend of theatrical and personal.

This book provides performers with a range of different female voices, which I hope you will find entertaining and fresh. When searching for an audition speech myself, I often encountered the same, familiar female archetypal roles and so, with this book, I was keen to provide a more satisfying feast of female parts from the very silly to the darker or melancholic. But mostly, I hope this collection helps you to find your inner clown.

A NOTE FOR PERFORMERS:

Ordinarily when preparing an audition speech it is necessary to read the full play to better understand the character and situation. These monologues exist in a vacuum – if you will – free of contextual restraint. I have deliberately not included a playing range or accent. I would encourage you, the performer, to feel free to create your own story and background to these speeches and decide on your own interpretation. They are designed as a vehicle for you to best show off your performance skills. The speeches within these pages should be approached with imagination and as a means of exploration.

I hope you find a speech that makes you laugh and that you will enjoy performing.

Good luck!

Katy.

A DIFFICULT YEAR

A woman enters with a pineapple.

Has everyone got a piece of paper!? Yes?! Great!
WHOOPPIE! *(She does a massive laugh.)* Don't mind
me! HAHAH. Oh, God – she's off on one – what's
she making us do now!? But seriously, has everyone
had a look at the pineapple? Said the actress to the
bishop?! *(Another big laugh!)* I've drunk on an empty
stomach – sorry everyone – what am I like!? *(Another
laugh.)* No, tell me. I want know – what AM I like,
hahah! Has everyone had a look at the pineapple?! I
won't ask again and has everyone got a pen?! Ok, Ok,
come on you lot – it's either this or I start singing…
*(She bursts into over-the-top opera and then laughs
again.)* HAHAH! I told you! Don't! Shut up! I've had a
drop…absolute chaos. Don't! Right, no, right, we're all
gonna go round one at a time and you've gotta write
down, listen, we're gonna write down how many leaves
you think are on the pineapple, no, listen, now come
on, now…how many leaves are on the pineapple.
Then I'll go away and count them and then whoever's
closest is the winner. Everyone, yeah? WHOOOPIE!
Hahaha. And that's it, that's the pineapple game! And
the winner…what does the winner get… *(Sung.)* *The
WINNER TAKES IT ALL.* Hahahh! I love musicals!
(American agent voice.)… "Kid – you got talent, make
sure you don't waste it". Hahah. The winner…I haven't
thought what the winner gets! I've got a sofa that
wants chucking- you can have that…how about an

extra portion of trifle and a feel of my arse. HAHAH. Right, COME ON EVERYONE – LET'S PLAY THE PINEAPPLE GAME! WOOOHOOOO! HAHHA, WHY IS MY HAND EMPTY – SOMEONE PASS ME A GLASS – WATCH OUT EVERYONE – …HAHAHA

The laughter slowly dies down and there is for the first time a palpable silence.

The silence is slowly filled with a wimper, an awkward, embarrassed, shameful sob then a couple of big sobs.

Pause.

Oh God I'm so unhappy…

She cries.

She slowly slowly pulls herself together. Her guests look on horrified. She clears her throat and composes herself.

I'm sorry about that everyone. I do apologise. It's been a bit of a difficult year I'm afraid…

Pause.

Right!

She starts counting the pineapple leaves.

One…two…three…four…five….six….seven… eight…nine…ten…eleven…twelve…thirteen… fourteen…

Come on everyone!

AB

I like sex. I'm good at sex. I don't think I'm a sex addict though. There is a website if you're in any doubt. They have a series of questions and if you answer yes to four or more then you have a problem. Well, it turned out that I wasn't a sex addict…but I was an alcoholic. But then I was drunk at the time – so I may have answered the questions incorrectly.

'Was I having sex compulsively?' it asked. No, I'd say it's more of a hobby than a compulsion. 'Have I ever tried unsuccessfully to control the amount of sexual contact I have?' With this body? It's not easy!

I'll tell you this though: I did once have sex to Alan Bennett. That's *to* by the way not *with*. I'm sure he wouldn't have minded. In fact, I think he would have been delighted. Felix, my ex – the impoverished writer, couldn't get to sleep unless he was listening to the sound of Alan Bennett's voice. He said it reassured him, helped him to feel sleepy and relaxed. So, there we were in bed together when he leaned over and kissed me, so naturally I went to turn Alan off but Felix stopped me.

"Don't you think that Alan Bennett sounds erotic?" He said. "I do".

"Well, I've never really thought about it" I said, "but I guess my instinctive answer would have to be, no. No I don't". He pouted.

"Well, how about we leave it on, anyway?"

"OK, fine", I said.

Well, it did nothing for me, but I still had a good time and certainly learnt a lot about the Mitford Sisters. It's always good to try these things. When it comes to the boudoir – I'm never adverse to experimentation. It's healthy and everyone knows I've been a creature of whim since birth!

It didn't last long after that. He did two things wrong:

1. He admitted to still being in love with someone else.

2. He answered his phone whilst he was still inside me.

Just a few weeks later, a friend of mine told me that she had spotted AB (Alan Bennett) in the vegetable section of her local organic fruit and veg shop, *Planet of the Grapes.* She said it took all the strength she had not to rush up to him to tell him that two people had made love to the sound of his voice.

We're no longer in touch, the ex and I, but I do think about him from time to time, and I wonder if he's listening alone or with company.

Just this morning, well, I heard Alan Titchmarsh on the radio and for the first few seconds I thought it was AB! I even considered getting back in touch with my ex to point out how alike their voices were. But I didn't.

I think Pamela was my favourite…of all the Mitford sisters, you know, but I wouldn't want to commit.

ALBERT'S LEGACY

Ah, no. Oh no, no, no – I'm afraid you're far too tall.
Oh dear.

Ah, no, you're too tall. It won't do. How tall did you
say you were on the phone, five nine? Five ten's my
cut-off point, I'm afraid. *(Calling off.)* Shut up Albert!
Well you may as well come in anyway and we'll see
what we can do. Watch out for that lamp! Worth a lot
of money. Don't make them anymore.

Could you stoop down a bit please? Stoop. Didn't
they say on the phone? I have a neck injury and I'm
struggling. I'm already struggling to look you in the
eye quite frankly. My neck just won't go any higher.
It might help if we could sit, but as you can see…my
chairs haven't arrived yet! Tuesday they said! I mean it
is naughty. Yes, we could *try* sitting down on the floor
all day like some kind of Japanese banquet…

She laughs.

I'm sure you'd cope just fine. I'm not sure I could even
get down there at the moment with this neck, let alone
get back up. We could sit on one of those packing
boxes I suppose but do be careful not to damage
what's inside. Ah, eye contact! There we are, very good
thinking. Were you a boy scout?

Oh, I loved it! I was a Girl Guide.

She lights a cigarette.

I would ask you first if you minded, but how would
you know you minded until I'd at least smoked
one? Ignore me – I've been saying that for years.
And besides, if you *did* mind, I'm afraid it would
rather be a problem. A fifteen-a-day habit comes
with the territory, wouldn't you say? As does all the
Victoriana…I collect it? Do you like it? You see that
piece there? It was given to me by my Grandfather.
People make the mistake of assuming it's a small chap
with a guitar when in actual fact it's a little girl and
a mandolin! They'll all need careful dusting. Let me
tell you a bit about the job. I've looked at your CV…
Now, I shall need to ask you at some point why you
left university after one year. I hope you're ready for
that question. I'm very much looking forward to the
answer. I do hope it's good.

But not yet, we'll come to that in a minute. Let me tell
you a little about the job and what will be expected of
you. You're general duties will include; walking Albert,
he's my Beagle, a few times a week for a gentle stroll,
as well as feeding him and giving him his medication
three times a day. I can't clean at the moment because,
much to my dismay, my arms are connected to my
neck.

Shopping's out as well…so you'll have to do that
too. And there's a lot more unpacking to be done.
Well you're sitting on most of it. My sister, bless her
did try and help me, but it's all in the wrong place,
silly woman. Still interested? The pay's adequate –
I'm a little impoverished myself. I'll pay you hourly,
okay? General dog's body, no pun intended. I'm not
interested in your political views or religious views. I
can see a church from the bedroom window – that's

my religious view – old joke – I've been saying that for years. Now, how about another cigarette…as dessert?

BEESWAX

(Addressing one of the mothers.) Would you excuse me just for one moment?

(Shouting off.) Can everyone just be aware that a jar of bugs *has* been spilt so please tread carefully!

(Addressing the mother again.) Sorry about that: our After School Science Club. Unfortunately for me, the emphasis is very much on practical this term!

Right, where were we Mrs Parsons, well I think that your daughter Rachel Parsons is a smashing girl she has a kind character but if I may continue Mrs Parsons, I think that Rachel Parsons has…I'm sorry, you're quite right: I *don't* need to keep using your daughter's full name, it is as you correctly say, superfluous. I think that Rachel and parents don't always like to hear this Mrs Parsons, but, I think that Rachel has gone as far as she can academically with us. Sorry, one moment…

(Addressing the pupils.) Claire! Claire don't become too attached to that earthworm will you – it's going to be returned to its natural environment remember…

(To the mother.) and so will all of you at half past thankfully…but – there's plenty to be upbeat about Mrs Parsons. Rachel has displayed other skills and interests in non-academic pursuits. For example in April she set up a Running Club and just last week in the staff room Madame Bertoli could be over-heard praising her jam rolypoly with the passion of

a thousand fires. So, there really is a lot of room for positivity here.

(To the pupils.) You're supposed to be writing things down remember girls! And remember to wear gloves if you dealing with any live and/or dead organic matter.

(To the mother.) Apathy, total apathy. They live their life through a screen don't they?

(She makes beeping noises and pretends to shoot people as if playing a computer game.) …that sort of thing. And as for the boys, I cannot begin to imagine what the effects are from such early exposure to pornography. What kind of model for intimacy is that for later life? There is a danger that they will expect all women they meet outside the virtual realm to be plucked and shiny with augmented breasts – and that simply isn't the case as you and I both well know Mrs Parsons. I feel I should apologise for that last remark Mrs Parsons: your torso is none of my beeswax! Interestingly enough, I once wrote a whole lesson plan on beeswax only to find that the Head hadn't approved it – she's not here today – she's attending Thatcher's funeral. My plan was to inform the children that they were all flowering apple trees and that I was a bee and that they were to all raise their palms in the air like so *(She demonstrates.)*. The bee, me, would then buzz through the classroom, placing my hand upon theirs, leaving a yellowy sticky residue – most likely egg or similar. Whoever is left with egg or similar on their hand HAS BEEN POLLINATED and will go on to produce apples – and those without, won't. The Head said she didn't think I should be touching, let alone fertilizing, the children's hands and that those who didn't get

pollinated might feel rejected. Ah well, half-term soon: dreamy!

(Studying the pupils wistfully.) One does wish their skirts were just an inch or two longer…

BREAKFAST

Look, the thing is…have your eyes changed colour? Oh my god…how did they do that? Mine go slightly lighter in the summer as well actually. Anyway, the thing is…I'm just not sure that you're right for me… it's not your fault…hey I like my men like I like my food: Chinese with pork balls. *(She laughs.)*

I'm sorry, what can I say?

It's not your fault.

All right, I'll level with you: you remind me of my father. As I said, it's not strictly your fault. At breakfast this morning you blanked me. I was standing by the cereals and I asked you if you wanted some juice and I smiled at you but you ignored me. And yet last night, you were happy to talk to me for hours; you were full of questions. I thought maybe we had a connection and then this morning – nothing. I feel like an idiot. And I thought…that's just what my father would do: push/pull, pull/push. Which is, maybe, why I was attracted to you in the first place? I'm sorry – I know this is intense. But seeing as you asked…well, that's the reason. You're probably one of the best-looking people I've ever met but you're inconsistent. I'm kinda sick of men like you and I'm sorry that you're having to take 'one for the team' here but do you know what I think you are? A seductive withholder. You seduce and then you withhold. You're like the 5:2 diet; it's all feast then famine. Once we've thrown our heads back in submission, laughing at your shit jokes, and you know you've won, then you subtly footstep away off to find the next unhunted buffalo in the room.

In this instance, just so you know, when I say buffalo I'm referring to females.

In fact, I kinda feel that's the only reason that we are having this conversation now: you can't be used to being turned down when you look the way you look, I imagine.

And who knows maybe it'll work out in the future. You'll get some therapy. I'll start doing meditation and learn to chill out and we shall meet again at a time when we have both become the best versions of ourselves. Who knows? Maybe we might even end up running seminars together for other couples and we coach them on how to achieve the same levels of intimacy and commitment as we have. Who knows? Hey, we could make a fortune.

But until such time, I wish you luck. It was nice meeting you and I look forward to meeting both of us in the future but until such time, goodbye.

CHARLES DICKENS

Question! If Charles Dickens were alive today would he be:

a) Writing *The Wire?*

b) Starring in *The Wire?*

or

c) Stumbling around, open-mouthed, vomiting with terror and astonishment at all the things he didn't understand about modern life?

Footnote: he was born in 1812, making him over 200 years old if he *were* alive today. He wouldn't be a pretty sight I suspect. His skin – what skin he had left – would drag behind him like a liver-spotted shadow. He'd also be in considerable pain. With hollow bowls of bone for eyes, he would occasionally look through the window of Curry's or Dixons where a 13-inch plasma screen is showing old episodes of *Everybody Loves Raymond.* He would force his 19th-century brain to try to recognize some semblance of storytelling and character as *he* understood it. But, as the episode goes on, it only seems to add to his genuine torment.

I think Charles Dickens and Charles Darwin were friends. Have I made that up? In the Venn diagram of their lives, the only overlap I can think of is Simon Callow who always plays them in bad TV films at Christmas.

All this new information on the man has lead me to set myself the challenge of reading the complete works of Charles Dickens.

This literary voyage shall begin with *Bleak House*. A cursory glance at page one, already informs me that it's pretty bleak. Whilst I am reading *Bleak House*, if honest, I suspect I'll secretly be wishing that I was doing something else like being on the internet, flaneuring, smooching or talking. However I have given myself a full year in order to complete this challenge, which does come with certain stipulations i.e. the man wrote about twenty-four novels for goodness sake…I'm not going to read them ALL. Some of them are non-fiction, one of them doesn't even have an ending (WTF!) and some of them look boring. I'm going to read all the main ones. Oh, yeah – and I'm allowed to give up at anytime.

(Said with American accent.) "And this kinda got me to thinking…" for those of you that don't know, that was my impression of Carrie Bradshaw, from *Sex in the City*. I think we are actually similar in style. By the way, if I was the Samantha Jones' character in the show, the neo-feminist/slag, depending on your politics, then at this point I would chime in with something like: "Well, I don't know about Dick-ens, but I do know about Dicks-out", before raising a perfectly shaped eyebrow and downing a pink gin.

The point is, I find reading novels has become increasingly harder, as the amount of possible things I could be doing increases. It takes a certain amount of discipline to – let's call it – 'read consciously'.

Does more choice actually make us any happier in modern life or does it simply paralyse us? Does *more* choice raise our expectaions perhaps? It could be a dangerous thing? Ergo – we are no happier than our forefathers (I only have one).

In conclusion: bring on the Victorian gloom. Whoooop!

ROUTEMASTER

My first ever job was working on a perfume counter.
I was nearly an assistant to a nit nurse but I couldn't
drive. I hated the perfume counter. I used to get a
stress migraine almost as soon as my shift started. And
I couldn't get used to living in the city; I'd walk around
with my bag clutched to my chest, thinking that I
was about to get mugged at any minute. Those weird
buses – the ones that don't have an end – they're just
open so you can see the road. What are they called?
Routemasters? I hadn't seen those before, but I started
getting really into them. Like every day when I got the
bus back, I'd wait for the Routemaster to come and
jump through the hole at the back and hop on. I don't
know why I liked them so much. I think it reminded
me a bit of when my dad used to take me and my
brother out in his pick-up truck, when we would ride
in the back, and watch the road dance and disappear
away from us. The hole was like a portal to the past.
But that day, I don't know, I guess I must have been
really tired or something 'cause I wasn't holding onto
the pole very tightly, and I remember that it was really
crowded, but I must have been too busy looking down
at the road, charmed by the two yellow snakes having
a race, because suddenly, just as the bus starts to slow
down, somebody nudges me and the pole slips away
from me. I'm floating out through the portal and
plunging towards the dark pavement and – bang! My
face smashes into the concrete. My bag, still clutched

to my side acting as a pivot point, as my cheek thumps to the ground. Everything goes everywhere. It's really embarrassing…make-up, my phone and bits of crisps; and all these leaflets about Irritable Bowel Syndrome… really embarrassing, but people were very helpful. They rushed off the bus and I think they thought it was a suicide attempt but, then when I opened my mouth, they heard how cheery my accent was and they knew it wasn't that. One kind lady came with me in the ambulance, which she really didn't have to. She gave me a marshmallow – her name was Audrey. My cheekbone had now swollen up to about the size of one of Kate Moss's…it did look rather splendid but it was also fractured. Three days later I went back into work at the perfume counter. They took one look at my black eye and big blobby face, and decided that there was no way I could work on the beauty counter, so I was downgraded to shoes instead. I was thrilled. I much preferred shoes with all the other weirdos. Shoes smelt of freedom!

EVE

An extremely nervous woman gets up.

Um…sorry, um, deep breath, *(She laughs.)* good afternoon…I just wondered *(She clears her throat.)* I just wondered what the… Oh I should say: it's a two-part question…is that allowed. *(She looks around.)* Um, yes…I…sorry…I just wondered what the panel…well, I, sorry…just trying to work out which question to start with…because the lady said that time was limited…just trying to…because they're both of equal importance.

Pause.

I've chosen…yes…sorry.

My first question is to do with moss. Um, we've had a moss explosion overnight and I was just wondering what the panel thought about it…sorry…the moss. There is some *very* anti-moss feeling on the internet but I think, well it's green, what's the problem really. It feels nice underfoot but it *is* messy. Messy moss. Mossy! *(She laughs at her own joke.)*

We have two bitches and the area where the bitches urinate is actually very lush and moss-free um…but the area beyond that where the bitches don't tend to urinate is, actually, very, as I have previously said, mossy.

Yes…um…the second question…no…it's gone. Oh, I've remembered. The second question, if there's time… Oh I did leave the room briefly at the beginning because I had a coughing fit (yes that was me I'm afraid – guilty), so this may have already been covered when I went out because of the coughing, so apologies if this has been covered…I am lead to believe it's a common problem, so statistically it may have come up. Um…good afternoon, sorry…I've said that. What is eating my spathiphyllum? Caterpillar or slug? The plant lives with me in my house but I do occasionally put it outside for a little holiday. It seems to do it the world of good. Having said that, I think this is when the insects take over. I have seen slugs in my house too, especially near the doors. I stood on one last week when I was having a wee in the night and I am not a screamer, I am not a screamer but well…as you can imagine…it was deeply disgusting. Can the panel help with all/any of the above, thank you. Sorry.

FIVE POUNDS

How can I lose five pounds by Wednesday apart from having a massive shit?

I'm serious. I'm going to be standing up there and making a speech in front of thirty five people and I couldn't even fit into my work bra this morning. Five pounds won't make me any happier, five pounds won't make me any better at public speaking, but it will give me cheekbones and everyone's more likely to take advice from someone with cheekbones: that's just evolution!

What's that Chinese thing that your sister did… those herbal teas that smelt of the forest floor? I tried laxatives once, but I took too many and I was in the chemists the very next day begging for mercy!

I am petrified of speaking in public – but I don't know why. At first, I'm fine. I'm calm. I know what I am going to say. I'm prepared. And then suddenly…I'm introduced: it's time, time to speak, talk-time and I'm weak and I lose it. I lose it. I lose it every time. There's only thirty five people, but it seems like a swarm and I can't stop my brain from chanting: no more, quit, stop, go, stop-it, quit-it, run to your Peugeot and be free, RUN TO YOUR PEUGEOT 208 AND BE FREE! All those peepers set on me and my golden complexion now white stone. Hands rattle in their pockets, mouth hollow, no moisture, no words, just a dry dead sound full of complimentary biscuits that have crumbled into angst. And Peter in Accounts won't think I'm hot anymore and Dominique on reception won't frank my mail anymore and David in HR won't put aside my jar of peanut butter like he always does, and I'll get over-looked and ignored, maybe even sacked and discarded like a worn out pair of shoes and I'll have to open that fucking bakery in Halifax back-up bullshit plan, and spend even more time with Mark, making holes in doughnuts that I can't even eat because I don't do carbs, and I know this is insanity on a Titanic scale but, if I could just shrink by an inch or two, and lose those five pounds and take up less space and have my very own set of model's cheekbones…by Wednesday…then…maybe, just maybe then…I could speak in public.

Oh, I've just thought…why don't you do it? What do you think? Oh go on.

FORTUNE

Peter was straight out of the army and we were looking for something to do so we bought an Island.

I said, "Will I hate it? Is it very over-grown?"

"Noooo", he said, "you'll adore it".

I said, "I won't".

He said, "You will".

I said, "I will not".

He said, "You'll adore it darling".

I said, "I won't".

He said, "You will".

So, I had a look and I adored it! I'm so lucky – Peter's always right.

Looking wistfully off and then suddenly bursting into song.

(Sung.) All Kinds of Everything Remind Me of You. Do you know it? It's our song.

(Sung.) Wedding bells, (Thinks.) Tunbridge Wells, la la la, la-la, la-la-la-la,la,la… Something like that – I never remember the words. It's not important. I don't like it that much anyway but Peter does.

Do you know Tonga at all? Such a friendly place. It's a modest Island – only a mile and a half. To put that into perspective, that's about the width of

Lake Windermere. Very friendly people the (*unsure*) Tongans? Tonganese? Tojan… Trojan? No.

We can't *really* though honestly, really, really honestly I mean really honestly possibly live there though can we Peter? He said, "What's the matter? Don't you want to wake up to the rustle of palm trees?" I said, "What's wrong with a silver birch?" Well he stood up tall and proud like a Norman tower and said, "I have lived through civil war, I think I can survive tropical storms, sharks, pirates and paw-paws don't you?"

"But what if there's a coup d'état? Have you thought of that? What if there's a coup d'état Peter?"

"I can't bear it when you speak French" he cried! And then he said something to himself in Latin – to spite me I think – he knows I dropped it for athletics. After all Peter thinks French *is* just sloppy Latin! I mean who speaks Latin now apart from doctors and the Pope. *(She laughs.)*

Pause.

(Sung.) All kinds of everything…

There we were in Wales. I adore Wales – we have a forest there – when he finally popped the question. He got down on the floor… I said, "Are you drunk?"

He said, "I'm sober enough".

"Enough for what?" I said.

"This proposal is the soundest thing I've done for years", he said.

"What proposal", I said. "Oh my god – are we in the middle of a proposal?"

23

I accepted of course with the following caveat: that the current Marquess of Salisbury's daughter, whose name I forget, was in the paper the other day flaunting a ring with a diamond the size of an egg and I felt I should never be truly happy again till I had one like it. And with that we shook hands.

I'm very lucky.

GIN

Never trust a woman with a small dark moustache. I certainly don't, if I'm being altogether honest, which I like to think I am. I mean on a man it's bad enough but on a woman, well, that's just…funny…and sad. By far the most interesting woman I ever met with a facial hair issue was my Aunt Camille. She was French but that's not her fault.

She lived on the outskirts of Paris in a beautiful apartment situated directly behind an abattoir. I spent a lot of my school holidays there, forever scared by the unmistakable pong of pig. But long-timer Aunt Camille had accepted the whiff.

Aunt Camille always wore summer dresses that were far too big for her. From the front, she resembled a large house. She had quite a trendy haircut for a woman of her age but, you know and a tash. And I always used to think; funny combination, funny combination, as you would.

Once, in the middle of the night, I found her sitting on the back porch, perfectly framed by a square of moonlight, overlooking the slaughterhouse.

She was crying.

"Aunt Camille? Is this about your mustache?" I asked. "Look, I've got a roll of sticky tape at the bottom of my rucksack – how about we use that to whip that fella off your face and we'll have you looking as smooth as the back of a spoon in no time."

Tears were now coming out at quite a pace. They fired down her cheeks like wet pellets.

"Il n'est rien de réel que le rêve et l'amour." She replied.

But before I had time to ask what she was on about, she promptly lifted up her dress to show me an enormous rash that went right across her belly.

"Oh my god" I say once out loud, once again in my head and then once again into a tissue.

(In a French accent.) "The doctors said it was the biggest they'd ever seen. The even took photos…I was humiliated".

She looked at me properly, for the first time. Mascara everywhere. Her eyes now resembled two crows trying to embrace.

"Did they give you any cream for it?" I asked.

"Yes", she mumbled. "They said it would go in a few days".

"Great," I said, "well, seeing as we're both up now, shall we crack open some of the duty-free gin"?

And with that, she squealed in delight, pinched her own cheeks and flashed me a smile whilst inadvertently showing me one of her fillings. A tissue was quickly spat on and then dragged across the two black puddles on her face. Then we sat on the floor, drinking and smoking till the rattle of the early cattle trucks announced time for bed.

I never found out what she was crying about.

GOGGLE BOX

I don't like the music that they play when a really fat person comes on the TV. It's always trombone music or something like that. Sometimes they will slow the picture right down so that all the fat really jiggles. I think it is cruel and demeaning. In my family we don't really watch those programmes anyway. We are encouraged to watch things about learning like maths or science. I don't think there will be a maths channel any time soon, but if there was, I would definitely watch it.

Also, in my family everyone is encouraged to be thin and healthy. We are not allowed things like Coca Cola or Frosties. I once had a bit of McDonald's in a car park and I told my mum and she was upset later. I like the history programmes too. I like it when they will show a baby in his cot and you can't begin to imagine what this baby has to do with anything – but then the man's voice on the programme will say "this baby grew up to become…Oliver Cromwell!" And then there is an actor dressed as Oliver Cromwell but he has now grown up to be a man and you're like 'oh ok, this is a programme about Oliver Cromwell. Cool'.

What is a bonkette?

I asked my mother if we could get a rabbit. She said perhaps. I said but when will you decide for sure? She told me off for nagging her and said that she would make her decision in due course. What does that mean

I said? May I have a date please? She said very well –
will let you know by Shakespeare's birthday. I had to
go away and look it up. The 23rd of April. That's in
two weeks' time! Cool!

In my family we play games like that so that you can
learn and actually know a bit more than before you
asked the question. I heard one of the other mums
saying that she couldn't shift her bonkette and I didn't
know what any of it meant.

Why did the pigs cross the road? Because it's up to
them.

I quite like cooking programmes, but there are far
too many thank you. They never seem to wear aprons
either and yet they are always clean. I just don't think
this is realistic! Plus they are always obsessed with
herbs.

I've wanted a rabbit for ages ever since *Watership
Down*, not the film, the book. It's obviously very sad
and I don't want to spoil it for you but one of the
rabbits dies. But what people forget is that actually
reading a passage in a book can be more haunting than
seeing a cartoon of it.

I've had something rattling around in my shoe all day.
It feels like a 1p. Would you excuse me – I'm going to
go and investigate…

GOLD

I'm not gonna lie to you: I've got a real thing about the Spanish. You know. I mean like proper. I love' em. I had one of those teach-yourself Spanish things on my IPod. Yes, I was learning it for someone in particular. And then the IPod got nicked and then the bloke got nicked, not even joking! Here's the thing though – at the end of the day – whoever stole that IPod off me, did me a favour 'cause I couldn't even trust him anyway. I should track that bloke down, what nicked it off me, buy him a pint and say thank you which is actually 'gracias' in Spanish, plus I got a new iPhone now, so I didn't need an iPod – I only used it down the gym anyway but they got MTV now instead.

Some days, my friends are like: if you think Spanish blokes are so fit, why don't you just move there? I've got one friend who works in a travel agents and she was like you can't just go for the blokes. She said it's a beautiful place…the culture…and I'm like, what beating up a bull in front of loads of people and she was like no, she goes no, like Picasso and…crab pots and everything.

The weather'd be good though. I think I like the skin tone and the dark eyes…and the accent, that and the Irish…OMG! I know they're not similar I'm not saying that!

Most blokes I meet though round here that are Spanish are gay…I see a lot of them coming out of that gay gym – oh my God – they look so fit. My mate Alex works there – he's not even gay, don't tell anyone – I'm not supposed to tell anyone 'cause he loves working there. But he just pretended to be gay to work there – he says he gets loads of perks – like he can use the gym and they got like a massive like communal steam room and a massive sauna which he can go in whenever he wants but he's not gay.

What's the Spanish word for 'gay'?

I think it's just 'gay'.

HAZEL

This diary belongs to Hazel Hoops, age thirteen. If lost please return to Miss Steiner's class, Bishop Gross Testi Grammar School.

Monday – the school bus broke down today outside an Ann Summers – everyone took photos on their phone. I ate three boiled eggs while the men fixed the tyres.

A policeman came to the school today to make a speech about drugs. He was anti them. Michelle Berridge says that all drugs are white. I don't know if that is true but I went along with it to keep the peace.

Tuesday – Did you know there are loads of Welsh people in Patagonia!?

Also Peter O'Neil has been germinating marijuana seeds in his sock.

One of the art teachers was wearing jeans today; everyone was talking about it.

Mr Boo retired, no one talked about it.

I saw Chris Lang climbing up the side of the boys' toilets. I fancy him. He looks even better when he's in the air. Also I wish I was in Gryffindor but deep down sometimes I worry that I'm actually more Hufflepuff.

I've grown an inch. Everyone's noticed.

Wednesday – badminton was cancelled, so we all had to throw beanbags into a bucket instead.

Only two hundred and four days left till Christmas, yaaay!

We're doing a project on China. Did you know that in the Chinese calendar each year is represented by an animal? And they believe that you always have some of the characteristics of the animal of the year you were born in. We all went round the class and said what animal we thought we were most like…I said a gnat.

Thursday – we made sausage rolls today. Mrs Bergmann said I had a soggy bottom. I said I liked mine like that though. She told me off for being cheeky. But what's the difference between being cheeky and telling the truth? She doesn't know anything anyway – she covers her front garden in elves at Christmas time and everyone reckons that the thing round her neck is actually a bit of placenta.

Friday – This is what you do if you want to measure out six foot, this is based on having size five-and-a-half feet though.

She paces out the distance by laying each foot out so that the back of one foot touches the front of the other with no space between the feet.

(Whispering as she steps:) one, two, three, four, five, six, seven, eight.

That's how you measure out six foot. Approx. There, I told you I know lots of things.

I caught some of the younger girls trying to contact the devil today. Needless to say it didn't work. I actually felt sorry for them, so immature. They were under a stairwell which is where a lot of stuff happens.

Saturday – Saturday morning is Music Club. When I grow up, I hope to be like KT Tunstall or Pink, but less aggressive. I've written a song called 'Yellow' but it's nothing like the Coldplay one, besides which I don't care.

Sunday – nothing happened. The End. Good night.

HOUSE HUNTING

Patterned glass, there.

Not really a pattern though is it? It's quite random.

Now, I know a red kitchen isn't to everyone's taste. I am aware of that. You could paint it green for example, green would be nice. My kitchen's yellow. But there are, as I'm sure you're aware, plenty of other colours to choose from…you could say it's not as black and white, as just green or yellow. *(Enjoying her own joke.)*

Listen. This is what I always tell people: first timers, *(Points to her ears.)* 'Clip-on'…yeah? 'Clip-on'…you know like clip-on earrings…

'C.L.I.P.O.N.'

Condition, Locality, Impressions, Price, Ownership and finally Next door, or Neighbours, if you will. Both words start with an 'n' so…

Clip-on; an easy little way to make sure you've asked all the right questions when viewing a property.

Now, the current owners, Mr and Mrs Hooper, she's an immigration lawyer… he's not, are looking for a quick sale…apparently there's been a death in the family. Oh, I've got that bowl, only in blue! So speed is of the essence.

Nice big kitchen…you can fit plenty around the table…are you thinking of starting a family anytime soon? No! Shouldn't have asked – none of my business.

Right, where was I? Ooh, can you smell garlic? Oh, it's probably me – I had a heavy lunch. It's a lovely little French place round the corner in fact. Beautiful – bit of a leaving do for one of the girls. She's off to Australia no less…for love! She met him on a bus! Weird innit? She's only known him 6 weeks. I said, 'Tess, he's got lovely arms, but are you sure he's the one'.

Oh, now this might interest you…you see that house over the road there?

That's where Enoch Powell grew up…there's no plaque or anything. Weird that isn't it, don't you think? A racist living opposite an immigration lawyer…well used to live…

I've got that wind chime…only mine's made out of bamboo.

IS STEVE IN?

So, like, you know how you said that you could hold your breath for four minutes, well I looked it up and David Blaine actually held his for 17 minutes and 3 seconds and that was underwater so like, no offence but four minutes is kind of not that that big a deal, so if I were you I'd stop going on about it, is all, because it's just not that impressive especially cause you're not even doing it in water and you've mentioned it like seven times since we've been going out, and we've only been going out properly for like three months, well four if you count the first month when we *were* going out but I didn't realise… so, you know, 'you do the math'. It's not a criticism, well it is, but…well there's no but…it's just a criticism.

And also, sorry to rant, but, that's not the real reason I came over here, there was something else that I… *(Suddenly noticing.)* Oh your cold sore's gone! Oh great, when did that clear up? Oh, good for you!

Yeah, I suppose that does mean we can start kissing again. Yep.

YEY! *(Trying to seem pleased.)*

Where was I? Right, yeah – the other thing. Well the other thing I had to say was, um…well…the thing is Steve…you eat with your hands!

Um, yeah, I don't know if you even realise you're doing it…but you do it all the time. It's pretty gross. I mean have you got a problem with cutlery, like a fear or…or maybe you have taste buds in you fingers…that would be pretty cool actually, anyway, it doesn't really matter, the point is, the point is…

I…just don't think it's gonna work out between us. I'm really sorry..um..but.. you know…

What?

Why? Well, what d'you mean, why?

Steve, you repeat yourself constantly, you've got facial herpes and you eat with your hands! Even Porridge! I mean it's just weird!

There. I've said it.

God, I feel better already, don't you? Wow, that feels so good to just get it all out there…you know?

Awkward pause.

Yeah, that's what a cold sore is, herpes, but on the face and stuff. Yeah.

I don't know if you're still allowed to wank, Steve, you'd have to ask your doctor…

Look it up!

Well, look, I better go but, you know…good luck with the fun run on Saturday and um…let me know about the wanking thing, oh no actually, I don't know why I said that, don't, don't let me know.

Okay.

Bye.

Bye.

Exit.

KINKS

So, I'm late. I'm late again for work and the thing is
I can't be late again. And this is the latest I've ever
been…apart from the time I never showed up. So I'm
running, running through the back streets of Soho
and there's all sorts of kinky shit in the windows on
offer and it's only the morning! And I haven't run since
primary school right, so I'm knackered.

And then I see it – a little sign in a window and it
just says, 'Have you always dreamt of having straight
hair?' And the thing is, I'm looking at it and I'm
thinking YES! YES, I HAVE always dreamt of having
straight hair. Next thing I know, I'm in the salon
and I'm telling this sweet little gay guy in a little vest
how I've always dreamt of having straight hair. Guess
how much though? Two hundred and fifty quid! So,
I'm like no way. And then the little gay guy goes *(An
attempt at a Brazilian accent.)* 'Oh, but you know baby,
this treatment, it's Japanese, is really really good. Let
me have a look at your hair baby, yeah baby I could do
that for you and then no more frizzy frizzy yeah – you
gonna look like a princess and your hair's gonna be
straighter than Tom Cruise'.

– How long does it last for though yeah?

– Baby, is forever.

She reacts dramatically.

(Stage whisper.) Forever!

38

No more photos on Facebook where my hair looks like a bag of smoke, no more getting up twenty minutes earlier to try and tame it into submission. OMG! How often in life do people's dreams actually come true? It's like I'm a little dying kid and this Brazilian guy is Noel Edmonds and it's Christmas day and we're on TV. That's what it's like. My dream has come true. I close my eyes and say 'yes' – and he says he can fit me in next week. And then I start thinking; but maybe it's wrong? Is it denying who I am? Is it messing with nature? And then I remember about The Apprentice. It's always the woman with the curly hair that gets fired first. Have a look, yeah. Truth. If I want to climb the corporate ladder, which I do – you gotta look right, gotta be taken seriously.

So, I get into work and they're just like looking at me like 'this girl is a joke' and they're all going mental and then I just start day-dreaming about having straight hair, cause that's what I do when people are shouting at me – I just think about other things. Seriously, what is wrong with me? I can't even pay my rent and I plan to spend two hundred and fifty quid on hair…

(Then, genuinely chuffed:)

Brilliant.

The End.

KITTY

Honey, I know money. I also know how I can help you out a little. Now, you'll need a pen for this, alrighty? If you have a pen, then I'll begin. And…you may want to be seated. What I'm about to say might shock you honey.

Please take this down:

Head along Fifth Boulevard then turn right at the pet store, then head left at the second intersection, are you getting this? Take the Six Thirty-Six to North station. You want Maddox Street – on the right. Now, you're looking for a small, plain apartment. Its only distinguishing feature is a large black wooden door that gets hot in the summer – number 47. The key will be stiff but persistence is key, do you get it? My father was a wit too. Then once inside, the first thing you notice are the bookshelves…where the books are stored. At this point you may want to stop and admire the thick pale blue and pink fine Persian carpet on the floor. It's the real thing honey, made by holy Persians and I went through holy hell to get it! As you ascend the stairs you may take this opportunity to admire the beautiful backdrop of photographs that evokes the mood of high-society glamour. Now, we're getting to the good part.

Once upstairs, you may enter my boudoir, which is the first door on your right. You got that? Make your way over to the elegant French iron bed. Now, here's the scoop – get down on your belly like a snake and slither your way under the bed. The first thing you'll see are some rolled up canvasses…I was briefly stepping out with an artist. It didn't last long. But he did so love to paint me nude. Oh don't look so shocked. Am I not blood and bone? It is, after all, just nature. The lace draped over my face has retained my anonymity but nonetheless they do the job. Take your time – have a good look at them. He was especially adept as bottoms I seem to remember. Now I want you to take them and sell them. They're yours. You'll get a good price – believe you me.

LOOK UP

She suddenly looks up, noticing something. High up on a wall. She studies it for a bit before deciding to maybe say something.

D'you think that's a Banksy there?

I dunno. I dunno how you tell. I don't know anything about it.

D'you think he's good? Banksy? My friend says all he does is borrow images off other people but I dunno…I dunno anything about it…

She looks around.

It's well random this innit…you and me haven't really hung out that much together have we just like on our own…yeah…it's alright, innit…

How d'you think they got up there then like to do it. Hey, wouldn't it be funny if they found out that Banksy had a helicopter and that's how he got it in all them high places.

So, I dunno like maybe d'you wanna go and see a film? With me, I mean. Not now, but like another time, in the future, I mean it's gotta be in the future innit, we can't go and see a film in the past, d'you know what I mean. There's an Odeon near me which is sweet…it's only about twenty minutes on the bus. They do that thing, Orange Wednesdays, so probably a Wednesday would be the best like, if you wanna do Orange

Wednesdays, it's two for one…but I can afford normal as well if you wanna do normal. The only thing is you can't bring your own food though – I tried, believe me I tried – there's no way they're letting you bring it in, man. But they do Popcorn, sweet kind and salted kind for freaks, what's that about? They got like Revels, they got Minstrels, they got Twix's but in a bag, they got Haribo as well if you're not into chocolate.

Looks up again.

D'you know what makes me think it's a Banksy? I'm not saying I know about it, I'm not, I'm just saying because it's rats. And he always does rats, big black rats and I think I know why…'cause rat is an anagram for art…. I don't know, I'm not saying I know anything about it…don't quote me on that 'cause I don't know him personally and even if I did, then I still wouldn't know that I knew him 'cause no one knows what he looks like, you know, so I wouldn't know. You could be Banksy and I wouldn't know. Oh my God – are you Banksy? Are you though?

Pause.

No, but are you though?

Pause.

Are you Banksy?

Pause.

No, but are you?

Pause.

Are you?

Pause.

Banksy?

LOVE

She lists all these things as if it's an inconvenience but she actually really enjoys it.

OK. Things you need to know about me!

Claims to fame? Yeah. I got loads:

I once got in a lift with Mel Gibson, I once got down to the last two for Big Brother, you can see my mum on Google images, um Charlotte Church went to my grandmother's funeral. Loads.

Things I'm scared of:

Right, again – could be here all bloody day: spiders, hospitals, baked beans, being alone, aging, flying, choking, lions, that someone's gonna break in…can we move on…I can actually feel my anxiety levels rising here…where's my Paul McKenna CD?

Do I have a party trick!?

Yes! Yeah – sniffing out men at parties who have girlfriends and then falling for them and then seeing a book in a charity shop called 'Why Women Love Too Much' and then bursting into tears. *(Beat.)* I can fit my fist in my mouth as well.

Ever said I love you and not meant it?

Yes. Once. To my Grandmother.

But that's not the biggest lie I've ever told. No that would probably be when I pretended to have a drink problem so that I could get out of some personal training sessions that I had already paid for.

What else?

Favourite smell?

Fruit.

Earliest memory?

Don't remember.

Have you ever won anything?

When I was eleven or something like that I won a competition to find a pebble that most looked like a heart. Mine was so bloody good – I found it on holiday at Camber Sands, looked for ages I did and then I saw it: it was almost a perfect heart-shape and smooth. The prize was shit – a pack of colouring pencils. I've still got the pebble though.

It may surprise you to know that I was once arrested.

But can you keep that to yourself – about the arrest. I might want to work with kids one day, or become and MP – or fly a plane for that matter.

What's the worst hair style you've ever had?

Probably this one if I'm honest…

MAY

Guess what they're turning it into? A bloody Starbucks. Why are those coffee machines so loud? It's like listening to a jet engine going off…I'd find it more relaxing to sip a cappuccino on the main runway of Heathrow. People today seem very angst-ridden to me. I'm not sure more coffee is what they need to be honest with you.

You should see some of the women from head office that come down here. Their hair is poker straight, so shiny and they always look like they've been dipped in egg white, slightly glazed. I don't know how you achieve such a look. Immaculate! Anxious though, they show up, unannounced and they move about the place with their notepads like a shoal of frightened fish. Well, they're just as worried about losing their jobs as the rest of us.

They've done just about everything they could to pump fresh blood into this place. The toilets are no longer just toilets, now they're 'a congruent sensory branding experience whilst undertaking a necessary daily function'. The idea is to recreate the outside inside, so now we've got these bloody great big pictures of dandelions everywhere, but it just looks to me like the seeds have been caught up by the wind and are gently floating into a sanitary bin. I'm not sure that's the look they were going for. Makes no difference to me, it's still a wall I've got to clean. I get it. I do. I heard Stephen Fry once talking on the radio. He's got a

46

lovely voice, hasn't he and he told a story about Oscar Wilde. Now apparently someone had asked Mr. Wilde why he thought America was such a violent place and he had said because their wallpaper was so ugly! But it does make sense to me, you know – there's not much nature left to look at is there…you could easily spend a whole day in this town without having seen anything green – apart from the Starbucks sign that is. And if you live in ugliness all day, then you'll feel ugly and do ugly things. It makes perfect sense to me.

An American man came in today and ordered a slice of apple pie but he left it. He didn't want it. Ungrateful bastard. So I wrapped it up in a napkin and put it in my handbag.

When I was little, my mother used to make the most wonderful apple pie. I'd always ask for second helpings. And then one day I stopped eating it and when she asked me why I said, 'I don't want apple pie, I want an apple pie life'. I don't remember saying it but ever since then, my mother would always say to me, "is your life as good as apple pie, May?"

Well, I'm still waiting for it to be. I'm still waiting for my apple pie life. I'm still eating it rather than living it I think. You never know, maybe the secret millionaire will come in tomorrow.

MOTHER

Hello. It's great to be here. I nearly didn't make it because of my depression. Um, I'm thrilled to be able to read out an extract from my book today for you all. It's part autobiographical and part based on my own life and it's really a follow up to my first book 'It's Not You, It's My Mother', and I think that anyone who has ever been, had or met a mother or indeed a father, son or daughter can relate to what lies within these pages. Could make an ideal stocking filler. So…without further ado I'd like to read an extract for you now from my latest book 'Womb For One More'. Thank you.

'It was nearly 4'o clock by the time the afternoon came round. I decided to walk to Mother's. As I approached the house, I could see her large melon-shaped head appearing from behind the front door. 'You're late', she cried, gesturing wildly with her hands so much so that they resembled two large pancakes, mid toss. It was pissing down and I wasn't in the mood. She knew I'd be late, I had told her, but nothing ever really went in to that melon-shaped head of hers.

We sat at our usual places in the living room. 'I'm on the blood-type diet' she announced. I thought to myself 'oh yes, and what is the dietry recommendation for a cold-bloodied hag like you, Magnum ice creams?' But I didn't say it out loud. She slumped back in her chair like an old tired lion in Uggs. I got up and opened a can of rice pudding and tried not to think about my depression. I asked her if she had a separate recycling bin to put the empty can in. She called me a hippy and lit up a fag. I put a lot of things in the bin that day – metaphorical and real – because it was bin day.

She picked up the clay pig from the Ikea Billy Bookcase. 'All this will be yours one day when I'm dead' she said.

– Please Mother, I don't like to talk about such things.

– Well, it's true isn't it, I mean we're not Egyptian – I won't be burying it with me.

I know we're not Egyptian, but still, so morbid.

We sat in silence for a bit. I fantasize about a giant fireball surging its way through the house, hungry for destruction and obliterating all the clay pigs and crucifixes that crosses its red-hot path.

We watch a repeat of Eggheads'.

Thank you.

MR STRIPES

'Well, what a sad day, what a sad, sad day. When Angela asked me if I would say something today, I was of course nervous… I didn't know Mr Stripes that well, and our paths only crossed towards the end of his life, but I took much away from our brief meeting…and just from talking to Angela and her children today it's clear that he was loved and cared for very much.

I suppose what first struck me about Mr Stripes was his wonderful black hair…beautiful black hair and those charming eyes of course, famed for them. I can just imagine him now – sitting on the roof, eating out of bins, chasing kids and playing with his bell. He will be sorely missed. And I hope that his brothers and sisters, um… *(Reading from piece of paper.)* 'Captain Kit Kat', 'Puddle Jumper', and 'Kiss Kiss', don't miss him too much as well.

Clears her throat.

When Angela asked me if I would do a poem I said 'oh no, don't make me do that!', but I was of course joking, 'it would be an honour', I said. Apparently Mr Stripes loved books and would often fall sleep on one…*(Little nod to Angela in congregation.)*

I wanted to read out the poem from that bit in *Notting Hill* – no, not Notting Hi…*Four Weddings and a Funeral* – when the loud gay man dies…but I didn't know what it was called and my internet's down…so I've penned a little something myself. So, here we go – a poem in memory of Mr Stripes. R.I.P. Thank you.

'Oh Mr Stripes,

you were a one,

coming through the cat flap

when your day was done.

I looked in the mirror

I'm sure that I did

I even tried to

swerve and skid

to avoid your little skeletal frame.

You dashed. I crashed. Your bones were smashed.

I'm surely to blame. I'm surely to blame.

I'm sure you're in heaven

Playing with some string.

If only I hadn't needed to go to Birmingham that day then I wouldn't have been driving'. The end.

Pause.

I couldn't find a way to make the bit about Birmingham rhyme.

So, apologies once again to Angela and family. I can only reiterate what a genuine error it was...

On a positive note – they managed to get the big side dent out of the car, so that's good.

Sorry. Thanks.

NINE DEEP

I am calm. I am calm. I am calm…but the thing is yeah…I've already got nine bridesmaids. D'you know what I mean? I'm going to be rolling nine deep when I go down that isle, d' you see what I'm saying: rolling nine deep…I got bridesmaids coming out of my arsehole. I'm sorry yeah but if that stupid cow thinks that she's gonna be bridesmaid too then she can suck my dick. I'm sorry ladies…I apologize to the rest of the queue as well – I don't normally wash my dirty linen in public but it's family innit.

Pause.

So Friday, we're in The Archers. I didn't know she was even going to be there and it's a shame you know 'cause we were rubbing along together quite nicely till this happened. In front of everyone she goes: 'What you gonna do with your hair for the wedding then? You should do a beehive like Adele.' I'm like, whatever 'cause I already know I'm doing half-up, half-down. And then she goes so you down the gym all the time then? I'm like – are you saying I'm fucking fat!

Sorry ladies, sorry for the language, but it's family stuff.

And the thing is yeah, he fucking loves his sister. Like he says weird shit like – she's the most beautiful girl in the world and I'm like – hello? I'm standing right here. I'm sorry but I don't fucking like her. And then the mum, don't get me started on the fucking – sorry

53

ladies – mum. First of all – it's her son's engagement party, not a scrap of make-up, sort yourself out luv. She got a weird forehead too. They all got weird foreheads – it's like…what's that word…Neanderthal. First thing I said to the sister was that she should get a fringe…I even offered to do it for her but she just done a face like she could smell something bad.

Is there someone in there still? Fukin' hell – she's been fucking ages in there – what's she doing – snorting half of bloody Columbia.

They're tight you know. Every picture on Facebook, she's hugging him all the time. I dunno, maybe it's me – 'cause in our family – we hug at Christmas and that's about it, you know, oh and if something has happened to one of the cats.

Knowing my luck…she'll probably turn up on the day all in white with a bloody veil on her head and try and marry him herself. Uuughgh.

Oi! Come on! What you doing in there!? IF I DON'T HAVE A PISS SOON I'M NOT GONNA BE ABLE TO HAVE CHILDREN…I'M DOING INTERNAL DAMAGE HERE!

PHILIPPA

Please, let me stop you there Professor. Are you referring to the passage in which I say 'I have always thought of the vagina as a chalice and the penis as a dagger'? I can tell by your face-smile that I'm right.

Guilty then. Guilty. I admit it. One has to ask oneself; was it an act of lunacy to think that I, Philippa Baublebaum could use a quote from one of the greatest scholars on early Medieval and Renaissance symbology and pass it off as her own opinion, thinking she could get away with it? Probably, yes. My fate now lies in your hands professor. Or should I say 'cups' – I hardly need to remind you professor that early-to-mid-medieval wall hangings always depicted hands as cupped like a half-moon.

So… "What studied torments, tyrant, hast for me?" Mmm?

I suppose you're wondering why I did it aren't you?

When I woke up on the morning of last Monday or 'Moon day'; the day of the exam, I had the strangest feeling; a combination of absolute terror and infinite calm…or to put it in medieval terms, somewhere betwixt 'phlegmatic' and 'choleric'. I am of course, professor, referring to the four humours of early medieval medicine.

It had been a night full of bad dreams; portentous visions of amulets and sabres, pageants and heraldry,

big angry babies and various horned god heads…all
of which I knew were bound to pop up in tomorrow's
exam…and subsequently did not. I couldn't not stop
worrying about not passing the exam…hence the
dream I just mentioned.

And yet here it was: the day of the medieval and early
renaissance symbology exam – and I, like those who
had studied before me, were to bend down and be
made to wear this great responsibility like a cape or
'cloak', as it was known back then, but sometimes
'cape' as well actually.

But as soon as I entered that exam hall and took to my
throne (chair), picked up my quill (pen) and began
to scribe (write, write down the answers to the exam
questions), I knew that I had definitely, definitely not
done enough revision. Of course when I saw little
Maddy Knockles faint under the pressure it provided
some welcome comic relief. Have you ever seen Maddy
Knockles faint? It's like watching a thing go faint and
fall over onto another thing. But this is my account,
not Maddy's! I knew I still had an ace up my sleeve:
my specialist knowledge – 'Medieval sex symbols as
used in ritual'. It was then that I had the idea. I have of
course read 'Vagina as Chalice and Penis as Dagger' by
Stephen Grab but I didn't think anyone would notice
if I pretended it was my own original thought. I did it.

After the exam, I went immediately to my quarters
and forced myself to drink Nesquick, which I hate, as
a form of punishment. I had to do a watercolour to
calm myself down but was so upset I thought I only
deserved to use the brown…so I painted a leather coin
pouch. It's actually rather good. In retrospect, was it
worth it – no.

POST

How can you sit there and say I haven't made any effort? I give seventy percent in everything I do. How can you say I haven't given it my all?

I love this job. I really do. I didn't straight away. I don't mind admitting that. I did struggle at first…I'd been on sabbatical…round at my cousin's, so I was a little out of touch with the employment world.

I remember on my first day when you told me what time I'd have to start getting up in the mornings and I nearly wet my pants laughing. Admit it – you never thought I'd last this long, did you? And it was a shock, oh my god – it was a shock to the body at first. 4am. Ouch! I used to think about the halcyon days of sitting on that sofa with my cousin, smoking menthols. So, yeah, I know I was crap at first. I know I was lazy, but these last few weeks, I swear something has changed… it's like someone's been tinkering away with my cogs… it was like a software update. The clock in my body stopped and reset itself to a different time. I went from being a night owl to an early bird. And now I'm part of the secret 4am club – just me and the pigeons and the piss-heads sharing the air. I love it now. Even on my days off, instead of lying in bed, I'm up; tick-tocking away nice and early. Just pottering or whatever, you know: productive. My cousin's like, 'why are you texting me at 10.30am in the morning on a Saturday, piss off'.

To be honest, before this job, I never stopped to think about how my letters got to me. I didn't really open them that much to be honest with you either. *(She finds this funny.)* I mean you don't think about it do you…same with milk, you just don't think about the journey. In my first week, I thought we'd get the day off because it was raining, but no – you've got to be out there delivering on your bike rain or shine.

This job has taught me about people you know. Because you gotta be nice, you know? I see it all: unpaid bills, final demands, the chaos at Christmas…a heart-shaped box on the Valentines. I see it all. You know those little red and white cards that say 'Sorry, we missed you'; well I draw a smiley face on mine, just to prove I mean it! I am sorry. I feel like I'm out of my cave, you know. I swear it's different now. You can't get rid of me.

A cat scratched me last week when I put my hand in the letterbox. It happened three times. I didn't even tell anyone.

RABBITS

Anthony? Anthony?

Anthony? Do you think there are enough Peter Rabbits out front now? Or should I get more? Anthony?

Pause.

Mmm, I think there are enough. It's hard to tell you see – sometimes, particularly with a lot of our Asian visitors, they are often disappointed that there aren't more Peter Rabbits, but then a lot of the school children will say that they feel quite overwhelmed by the amount. It's hard to know who to please really. And of course we're constantly competing with the Pencil Museum, which is only about twenty miles South West. *(She points in the direction of South West.)* Oh actually *(She does an embarrassed laugh. Correcting herself, she points in the opposite direction.)* Sorry! South West. So, it's important that we…Anthony! I can see a Little Pig Robinson out here without a jacket on, but all the others have jackets on, is that right?

He's busy.

Anthony's my brother. And I'm his sister.

He's older than me by three years but people say we look about the same age, which is fine. Yes, we do get a surprising amount of overseas visitors, which really does act as an enduring reminder of Beatrix Potter's universal appeal. And some people say she didn't like foreign people and that just isn't true. Anthony? The rubbers are arriving at four – you haven't forgotten have you?

He's busy.

We were just like that as children…we've always been close. People aren't surprised when I say we work together. I say it's like Richard and Judy, oh no, they're married aren't they, um, The Carpenters – they still work together don't they I think. Speaking of carpenters… *(Nervous laugh.)* Anthony! You know the bench that people sit on to have their photo taken with Mrs Tiggywinkle and friends at the end of the attraction, well, it's not there…d'you think the coffee shop borrowed it because of that coach party?

He might be listening to Mariah Carey. He does that when he's stressed.

She has got a powerful voice. I love her Christmassy songs. She does seem a bit odd though. I said to Anthony well if you love her so much then why don't you write to her and ask her to make a special appearance at the One Hundred Years of Peter Rabbit Event and he actually did! We didn't get a reply. We get a lot of Americans, I think she'd probably love it, she'd probably write a song about the experience. I don't think she'd fancy Anthony though. He's got a face like half a grapefruit.

Would you excuse me, the rubbers are here.

RACHEL

I've got and audition for *Doctor Who* in half an hour…I'm like this …*(She holds out her shaking hands.)* I'm like… *(She does a raspberry to indicate that she is shitting herself.)*

She laughs.

It's not to play The Doctor, obviously…we all know who the part went to in the end. No, I think Peter's a great choice, I really do. It's old school, innit – having an grey-haired bloke again as The Doctor. Brilliant actor, brilliant actor. But when it was announced on that programme, I could just imagine fourteen year old girls up and down the country bursting into tears of confusion 'cause they didn't fancy him, d'you know what I mean? Brilliant actor though.

No, it's a return to form. I'm up for the part of Empress Nargoose. Great little part. I'm in episode three and then again briefly in five when she transforms into a toxic puddle. It's quite a challenge because the top half of my face will be covered…and the bottom half…as well as my entire body, so it will be quite demanding but that's ok because I think the reason I was chosen for this audition was because the director saw me in a short film last year when I was playing a woman at a cash point, in a burka and I was being robbed but I only had the use of my eyes you see *(She frames them.)* to express just how frightened I was, so I can fully understand why I'm being considered. I don't have to play the puddle as well, that'll be special effects or an actual puddle or whatever…

I've got my mum staying with me at the moment. She's not very well to be honest. Whatever tablets she's on, they're giving her terrible wind. Her farts are so loud – I think someone's calling me form the other side of the house and I come rushing in…

Mum loves having a daughter in show business. Oh yeah. I've been acting since I was tiny you see. Oh yeah.

I once had an audition for this comedy show right. Like a sort of late night satirical thing. Anyway, so they hand me this piece of paper and this woman in a poncho goes 'You'll be reading for the part of dragon two'. So, I'm like right, okay dragon two great. SO, I get in there and I just go for it. I do a welsh accent and everything because that seemed appropriate you know and I'm breathing fire, got me talons like this and everything and they're sort of enjoying it. They look a bit freaked out and then I suddenly realise that it's a spoof of Dragon's Den so rather than stop what I'm doing I very slowly try and turn the dragon into a Deborah Meadon impression. It was actually a surprisingly smooth transition. Didn't get it, but, you know – showed off my versatility, so, every cloud and all that.

SOUP

May I speak now?

Well, I shall be making my pea and ginger soup tonight. I've been making it for over fifteen years! Sainsbury's do frozen organic peas now – it's changed my life! Wonderful. Joanna and Simon are coming over, in fact I'm expecting a call from them any minute. And she...do you remember, she...now you've heard of Lord and Lady Falkland haven't you, as in the Falkland Isles you see – which I know you know about because we covered the Falkland's War, didn't we when we were revising for your British citizenship exam? Well Joanna used to live next door to Lord and Lady Falkland and Joanna said that Lord Falkland was a lot of fun and that one day he went round and he cut a very small hole in the door in Joanna's bedroom so that her dolls had their own little entrance, they're own little door you see? And then they had a son, I can't remember his name it was a name...like...Felix... Duncan – that was it! Well, he went onto play Sweeny Todd in Leeds.

Do you have a whizzer? Remind me.

Um...*(She mimes blending soup with a blender.)*

Um...I don't know how to say it...blender? ...I don't know...um. Like oh like 'robot da cucina? Si! Si!

Well, it makes the whole thing much, much quicker. But, listen! What I do is, instead of tarragon I use marjoram, instead of cumin I use caraway seeds and instead of peas I sometimes use fish.

Now, we have two choices: we could go and do the food shopping now OR, listen, we could wander down...we like a bus don't we? Yes, we like a bus...or we could wander down, pick up the 159 in that case grab a coffee, and then end up back at the market? Oh and by the way I don't think I'm going to make your birthday celebration on Saturday after all – it's the day of the gallery opening and I just don't think I'll have any energy afterwards I'm sorry...besides you know what I think of your place – all that decomposing flora...I don't know how you breath...Now listen don't give me those cow eyes...

(Getting quite emotional and cross.) I'M SORRY BUT I SHAN'T APOLOGISE! YOU KNEW BEFORE GETTING INVOLVED WITH ME WHAT MY LIFE WAS LIKE AND I HAVE ALWAYS SAID TO YOU THAT MY LIFE IS AN OPEN BOOK BUT I DO HAVE A LOT OF FRIENDS. I DO HAVE A LOT OF SOCIAL ENGAGEMENTS, I AM IN DEMAND AND YOU KNEW ALL THIS SO PLEASE DON'T BE SURPRISED...

(Suddenly noticing.) Oh, how long has my phone been on silent? Joanna will be trying to get through...can you put it onto loud for me please light of my life? No, not loud...normal...no, vibrate, yes put it on vibrate. I'm more likely to notice a thing if I **feel** it rather than hear it.

TASTE

She watches TV.

What? You think Madonna is fit? Is that what you just said? You think Madonna is fit? No, you just said it. I heard you. You said, "Madonna is well fit". That's what you just said. Yes, you did. I heard you say it loud and clear. If there was anyone else here then I would have witnesses. If we could go back in time now and then I had a Dictaphone concealed in my pocket or something then I would press play and then there would be the sound of your voice going "I think Madonna is fit".

Whatever man. Just let me watch this in peace…

Pause.

So you think Madonna is fitter than me then? Is that what you're saying? Is that what you mean? You got something to say? You wanna say it to my face? Are you saying I'm ugly?

She returns to watching TV.

Why don't you go and dip your wick in Madonna then, yeah? Go and dip your wick in Madonna if you think she's so fit. She's obviously like the fittest person you've ever seen, so why don't you go and dip your wick in *her*! 'Cause you're not dipping your wick in me tonight, I'm telling you now!

Pause.

What If I asked if I could go part-time? That way I could spend three hours a day down the gym like Madonna does and then maybe I would look like that. I'm sorry that I can't spend three hours a day down the gym. At least I go to the gym. I don't see you going. It's bad for you anyway doing that much exercise. I know a woman who did a 10k run, yeah and her pelvic floor fell out.

(To herself.) Madonna.

It's stuck in my head now. I wish you hadn't told me. It's like that thing when people say 'don't think of an elephant'. I got you and Madonna stuck in my head, now. It looks wrong. It looks really wrong. She's old enough to be your mum.

I know how to make this even. I'm gonna tell you who I fancy, ok?

Pause.

NO ONE! BECAUSE I AM A GOOD GIRLFRIEND!

You didn't even know what an avocado was until you met me. You said it yourself – that I bettered you. That you were lucky to have me and that being with me was like being in a film, a good film, a film that you would watch in the cinema but then also get it on Blu-ray so that you could watch it over and over again.

You got some weird taste you have.

Madonna wouldn't go out with you.

Madonna would pick me over you. Yeah she would because she's bisexual. She would definitely go for me. No question. If Madonna came in here now and I said, "Madonna, my boyfriend wants to dip his wick in you, OR you can have a go on my tits, what do you think she'd say?" She'd be like, "I choose the tits". She would choose the tits option. You know it, and I know it. And then we would have some avocado and laugh at you!

THE ARRIVAL

I got home about seven o'clock, which is a bit later than usual. I usually get home about ten past six but I was running late that day because I'd got caught in a shower…I don't mean as in rain, no, I work at Homebase and I'd been showing a customer our new bathroom range when I got stuck in the shower cubicle. Yeah.

Anyway, so I get in and I'm always bursting for a wee when I get in, right, I've got a famously small bladder. My Nan says I've always been the same – I was like that when I used to come home from school. Which is weird if you think that now, I'm surrounded by toilets all day at work…but they're just for show – you can't use the shop ones. There are normal toilets too though obviously, for the staff…or that would be illegal otherwise.

So, *our* toilet is downstairs behind the kitchen right. So I go in and that's when I see it: the loo is full of something. At first I'm sort of rooted to the spot really, 'cause I mean I don't know what it is but I think, well I've got a pretty good idea of what it is but, I look again and I notice it's a really weird colour; a sort of pinky grey. Well the first thing I think is 'Oh God is Steve ill?! Because whoever's body that came out of… that is not a well body' but I go a little bit closer and that's when I realise…it's sausages…raw sausages… down the loo.

And, well, I just started laughing really, really laughing like it's sort of a release…it feels good. Why the hell are there sausages down our loo? Steve has heard me laughing from the other room and he's come in now and says 'what is that?' and I say 'it's sausages' and then he starts laughing too 'cause I'm still laughing as well.

And then I see the window and I work out exactly what had happened which I was almost sad about, you know, like it could have stayed as one of life's little mysteries. I had left a note for the butcher saying that we would miss the delivery and could he just pop it through kitchen window – 'cause where we live, you can do that sort of thing. And then it all made sense – well he just obviously got the wrong window.

Still – they were really tasty.

The End.

THE BOOK GROUP

Sorry, just quickly, before I forget, has anyone seen a blue jumper? I think I may have left it here last time. Can everyone just have a sort of quick root around for it…sorry…it's sort of light blue and well, turquoise I suppose if you were going to be fussy…and it's got the word 'Stockholm' embroidered across the front. The funny thing is I actually got it in Holland *(Laughs.)* not Stockholm as you'd expect! Long story…

No? Nothing? Not to worry, okay not to worry, I may have left it in Ryman's. I'll check on my, ooh! What's that under your chair? Oh no, my mistake, sorry John, as you were, sorry…

Well, I have to say, I was really disappointed by the book, I know, I know. I'm going to be the unpopular one here because everyone else clearly loved it *(Another nervous laugh and mimes strangling themselves.)* but no, seriously, for me, I'm afraid the character of the fishmonger was just totally unrealistic I'm afraid, um, my father bought and sold fish all his life and I didn't recognize any of the scenarios that were described in the book. So for me, very well written, but – um – the author obviously hasn't researched her subject which, to me, is just lazy…so for that reason, I would say 3 out of a possible 5 – would have been a 4 if… well I would have liked just a bit more care, bit more attention to detail…um…failed to 'reel' me in I'm afraid, pun very much intended, not a strong enough hook! *(Laughs.)*

Mm? Sorry?

Oh, what was he then?

A blacksmith?

Ahh *(Laughter and embarrassment mixed together.)*

Ah, well that explains that! Um… I don't know how I missed that. So he wasn't a fishmonger then.

Right… A blacksmith…

Right, I'm just trying to work out where I would have got fish from…the son isn't? Yes that's right, the son keeps fish doesn't he, that's right. Sorry, I got confused. I was thinking about the son.

Well in that case: 5! Top marks, because the bits where he was doing all the blacksmith stuff were spot on, was like being in the room. It was brilliant.

Now, because I can't make next week, would anyone object massively if we did *Watership Down* then?
I've read it so many times and I think everyone here knows my opinion on it. Would that be okay? Thanks everyone.

Blacksmiths…I don't know how I managed to miss that…I've been under a bit of pressure this week…a friend of my uncle's spontaneously combusted at a barbecue last week…so yeah…

THE BOSS

Richard, Richard, Richard, Richard, Richard, Richard…oh sorry, it's Michael isn't it, sorry Richard, I mean Michael.

I just don't buy it mate, I'm sorry, I've really tried to get my head around this…for weeks in fact.

I don't have the science to back it up – it's just instinct mate. And in the office environment, as any animal will tell you – instinct's all you've got.

I've read your personal statement Richard – MICHAEL – which I appreciate you writing, I really do, but I just don't buy it. I think the fact that you have tried to justify and explain your actions is highly…um…I know exactly the word I want…I just can't think of…well is in your favour…ADMIRABLE! That's the word I wanted. Highly Admirable, but you see that's the problem. I don't think it adequately excuses what you did – it's the explanation I have a problem with if you like…as I said, I don't profess to be a woman of science – I've got more of a sales background – but it just doesn't make sense. There's an expression the Native Americans' use which is '*all hat and no cattle*' that's what I think you are, Michael – I think you've got a great hat, but no livestock to speak of.

You say it's a new drug on the market, so perhaps they will discover more about it in the future, but for now, Michael, I think you have shown some aggression in the work place and I know there was an incident in which you hid some spoons. I've not been given all the details but, and as I said, I don't know whether perhaps you have had a reaction to this medication, but you're certainly not being yourself so I think maybe some time off would be advisable. Take some time off mate. Relax a bit and we'll see how you do…one of the girls said you like painting…doing a bit of art and that, so there we go…that's definitely something I would encourage. I quite like that Jack Vettriano myself. Michael, you've gone very pale is everything OK?

THE TOUR

So, if you'd all like to gather round…

Now, as you enter the village, the first thing you'll notice is that it appears to be falling into the sea. You'll know this because you'll see the big signs everywhere saying 'Danger, Danger', 'Enter at Own Risk' and 'This Village is Falling into the Sea'. So, how do we know this is actually happening? Well, in my case, I woke up one morning and usually upon waking all I ever get is… *(She does seagull/bird noises.)* But on this occasion it was more like… *(She is silent for a moment.)* Silence. No birds. I thought to myself, well the birds are quiet this morning…I'll go and put some more bread out on the bird table. Opened the back door, no garden: it had fallen into the sea. It was that quick. Starting to get the picture now? Yeah, it's not easy. It's not easy to live with: the constant threat of falling into the sea. And rain? Oh, we dread raindrops – oh don't get me started on rainfall. More rain means more soft mud which means more slip-sliding about. Now, what else can I tell you about…well for those of you that drove here, you'll notice the big holes appearing in the road, yes? Well, that's not the council that's coastal erosion that! But we can't do anything can we? You can't fight the elements. Who can you blame? You can't get a lawyer involved; you can't be all like, *(She mimes being on the phone.)* "Oh hello? Is that Mother Nature? It is? Oh great. I'm suing you. Please can you put all other natural processes on hold and be in court first thing, thank you!" *(She hangs up carefully.)* You just can't do it can you? Obviously you do feel that you're in a very precarious position. In a bad storm, it can be extremely scary. Occasionally, you might hear a loud 'plonk' noise as another bit of cliff drops off into the sea. It's like living with a horrible skin disease; I check the cliff edge every morning to see if another bit has flaked off.

I don't have a particular large frame, right, and I never remember my dreams, but my god last week I had the most vivid nightmare…seemed so real. I dreamt I was walking Abracadabra, my beagle, right, this is a dream now, not real life…I was walking Abracadabra through the park when all of a sudden I fell through the ground, into the sea and I was captured by the big fat octopus witch from the little mermaid cartoon and poor Abracadabra was turned into a seahorse. Now if that's not a sign of stress then I don't know what is to be honest.

THREE MINUTES

I like sitting in my garden. I can sit there for hours sometimes, smoking, reading, eating, sleeping and farting. I read my National Geographics. I like to read about rainforests, polar bears, Natterjack toads and adventures. Places I've been to are Brazil, Brunei, Florence and Canada. I'd love to go on a cruise but I'm scared I would come back fat and poor. Sorry about just now when I said I fart a lot in the garden. I personally don't have a problem talking about it. I've been subscribing to National Geographic for years… my magazines are very precious to me – sometimes I like to pretend that I'm the only person in the world that knows they exist – like I discovered them and I think that my eyes are going to stop working because I've stared too long at snaps of blue-bottles and articles on ocean innovation. It's hard to say ocean innovation…but I know really it's not just me who reads them because it has a global circulation of about eight million.

Do you want hear a joke? Mmm, I thought as much… sorry I don't know any. I like talking, sorry you may have noticed. I do rabbit on. Speaking of rabbits, the Aztecs used to worship a group of four hundred rabbit gods…they must have spent all day on their knees… like a carpet fitter.

Maybe just put your hand up if you get bored. They once had this article about a frog that gave birth out of its mouth. The female amphibian, after external fertilization by the male, would swallow its eggs, brood its young in its stomach, and eventually give birth through its mouth and I thought…well that's a lot like me in many ways. I can't actually physically give birth through my mouth obviously; what I mean is that I find, well, each thought I have is like…an egg, say…so I'll have a 'thought-egg' and then I digest the 'thought-egg', incubate, allow it to develop until the time is right to give birth to a sentence…each word falling from my lips like a droplet of froglet to see if it will survive out there in the world without me.

Well, that's the bell. That's it isn't it? What happens now…do you move or do I? I don't know – I've never been speed dating before.

TOILET

I woke up this morning in my own bed. That's not the
unusual part. It's going to be a good day I think. The
sun shines gold onto my face through the curtains. I
stand. My legs feel heavy and hung-over…probably
because I am hung-over. Never try and put tequila in
your eyeball. I get ready for work and leave the house
on time.

Twenty minutes into my journey, I'm forced to dive
into the public toilets at Paddington Station because I
think I'm going be sick. Never try and snort peanuts.
Have you ever been into the toilets at Paddington?
They're decorated like an old hat box or a grubby
ice-cream parlour from the 1950s; all faded pinks and
cream stripes. A bit like someone in the future has dug
up the set of *Loose Women* and tried to restore it to
its former prime-time glory. As I wait in line, nursing
my distended bladder, sore eye and burning nostrils,
I notice that someone has graffitied something on the
wall to my right it says, 'to play toilet tennis, look left'.
So I look to my left and someone has kindly written
'to play toilet tennis look right'. So I passed my time
in the queue by playing toilet tennis for a while, then
went in to a cubicle, locked the door behind me,
placing my umbrella and big leather bag up on the
hook. The hang-over is starting to pass perhaps. I turn
around to see if there is any loo roll and that's when I
saw it.

Pause.

A human hand.

On the floor.

Just a hand. I was on my own, faced with this terrifying image. I could see every lurid detail of the man's flesh. I think it was a man's hand, open like a cup. I could see the line of head and heart. Chubby. Cold. Dead.

I left the cubicle backwards and was sick in one of the basins. The attendant woman couldn't wait to come over and start railing into me. I made a noise like an animal and she looked unsettled and shuffled away. I wiped my mouth and turned back towards the cubicle. Why was this happening to me? I am hungry, hungover, tired and now I've just seen a hand. Brilliant. I take a few deep, steadying breaths before once more pushing back the cubicle door, hoping to just see a nice bit of floor containing no human hand. But my whole body knows it's going to be there. Oh God! There it is. Oh No, I was right. There's the hand… oh hang on, it's just a glove. It's just a glove! Whoooo! It's just a glove. It's alright. It's alright, you're OK – it's just…a…glove. Big sigh.

And that was my morning.

TOO MUCH

She clearly remembers everything very clearly but is pretending otherwise.

I want to talk to you about what happened last night.

Pause.

What did happen? I genuinely can't remember a thing. I drank too much for my weight, age and height clearly because I remember very little. What did happen? I mean, I remember that we were at Ruby's Bar. I remember that obviously. But you weren't there then were you, no, that's right, you came later. Yeah, that's right. And we were all sat in a booth for a bit weren't we?

And then there was the dancing wasn't there? I remember that. Ha! I thought my back was hurting this morning. I was probably doing that wiggly thing with my hips again wasn't I? Yeah. Someone told me it was really seductive once, I think that's why I still do it. I don't really remember much after that though…

Oh and then we went to that bagel place, do you remember that? Oh yeah, that's right, because we ate ours in the gutter didn't we, just the two of us and then you were saying something about something to do with – it's hazy – but something to do with your fiancé and how you were having – guess the word would be 'doubts' about your wedding next week. Good luck with the wedding, by the way. Oh God, I feel awful. I must look awful. I get a really puffy face the next day when I've been drinking…

God, yeah and then the rest is just blank and I don't know. I've got this vague feeling that I may have said some stuff to you about having feelings, just stuff about feelings, having feelings for you. Yeah, anyway, look, you know – I don't remember any of this as I said…um… I think you may have responded? I can't be sure…flashback of you punching me on the arm and saying I was a great girl. It's all very sketchy. But really I just wanted to just try and piece it all together, so thank you, it's been really useful talking to you. I think I may have touched you inappropriately…um sorry if that happened. Ok, good.

Good. Looking forward to the wedding as well by the way. Good.

TRANSCEND

If I truly, truly loved myself then I would go to the
Antarctic. That's what I saw. During the bit where we
had our eyes closed and you asked us to imagine what
life would look like if we truly lived every moment, as
if we were good enough right now, and then you said
'where would you live if we truly accepted ourselves
right now' and that's where I was – sharing the air with
a penguin. I never realized there were worlds within
words before… I don't mind the cold…perhaps it's
a calling. I'd survive I think – I know a bit of Morse
code.

I saw other things too. If I truly loved myself then I
wouldn't be wearing this. God no. No! I'd be one of
those girls that only shops in vintage places and charity
shops, and I'd get notifications from eBay about
jumpers. My look, in summary – would be French
student from about 1995. People would say, "Did
you see that really cool girl at the party last night?"
"Yeah, you mean the one who looked like a French
student from 1995 or something?" "Yeah, she knows
something we don't about how to live, love and shop
and I wanna be her, or be near her". I'd have quite a lot
of impact.

If I truly loved myself, then I would eat better, exercise,
sleep better, work less, say no when I mean no and yes
when I mean yes and I'd live in the Antarctic? That's
what my subconscious seems to be telling me… I
dunno, I think I'd miss taxis. Did you know that the

word 'taxi' is like the same everywhere in every country or something…like…that? Closely followed by 'coke' and 'OK'. Sounds like a pretty good holiday to me. What's the international sign for thumbs up? I mean… is thumbs up an international thing?

Dash – dot – dash. Dot-dash. Dash. Dash – dot – dash – dash.

That's my name in Morse code. I don't know if it will be useful to me once I'm there: it's only really works if the person you are communicating with also knows Morse code or they will just look at you the way you're looking at me now. It's a dying form of communication…like Welsh. What do they speak in the Antarctic…Innuit? All those words for snow. No thank you but at least I'd know the word for taxi…it would be taxi. I don't know what happens if you want a taxi in the middle of the Antarctic, I guess a sledge and some huskies would come round the corner.

If I truly loved myself I would probably be taller, because I would walk around with my head up to the sun like a little bud. If I truly loved myself then I probably wouldn't have come on this course, no offence but I wouldn't have needed to, would I?

WATCHING

She notices something a few feet ahead of her.

Fuck! Oh fuck! Shit.

Without taking her eyes off the thing she is looking at, she shouts.

Wait! Wait! Don't come out!

She slowly moves about, trying to test out if it is safe.

Shit.

(Calling off behind her.) Chopsticks Collins is out here! Well I dunno – he must of escaped! I know baby! I know you hate dogs – that's why I'm telling you: pin back your ears yeah, Chopsticks Collins is out here. What? I dunno what time it is, what's that got to do with it?

She claps her hands together and tries to frighten him.

Shoo!

Shoo!

I'm trying to shoo at him baby. Shoo, I said shoo not shoot. What are you chatting about – like I'm gunna shoot Chopsticks Collins. It's not his fault. It's not your fault is it Chopsticks. It's that stupid owner of yours, innit. He can't be bothered looking after you properly can he? That's why he's always like this. He's just fucking ravishing. *(Beat. She realizes this is wrong.)* Ravenous.

She suddenly springs back.

Oh shit.

It's alright baby! It's alright.

He's just bearing his teeth at me a bit is all.

You know what the owner does, that guy – he works in a massive biscuit factory innit. Can you believe that – he hasn't even got a few spare biccies for Chopsticks Collins. That is pitiful. You know what we need? We need like a big steak, like in cartoons. I don't mean for us, I mean for Chopsticks Collins, to throw at him as a distraction. *(She starts clapping again.)* It's not working baby – he's not going anywhere. I'm not being funny but it kinda looks like he's smiling. Maybe he thinks I'm giving him a round of applause.

What!? No baby you already asked me that and the answer is the same: I, the time, do not know!

He looks like he's gonna be sick or something…

Baby! I can't believe you're bringing this up now. I just forgot to wear it, is all – don't be silly baby I love the watch; I just forgot to wear it today OK. I can't believe you're choosing to talk about the watch now! What's the first thing I said when I opened it? I was like I love this watch. You even found me one with the date in it and everything, didn't you, and with the numbers instead of when they just have little lines – 'cause you know I hate that when they just have little lines instead of numbers – it slows down my time-telling and you did all that for me didn't you? And – d'you remember what you said baby? You said that you had spent hours and hours just trying to find the right one and that you knew; you knew that it had to be a bisexual one.

Beat.

Unisex – so that if I died, then you could wear it too, so that you'd never forgot me and I thought that was the single most romantic thing I had ever heard.

I'm not being funny but Chopsticks Collins is being sick but there's nothing coming out. He's just going like this. *(She does an impression.)*

She laughs.

He's lying down now baby. Reckon he might sleep. Reckon we might live another day. He don't give a shit does he? You get to do what you want innit Chopsticks. You're the boss of you, innit. I admire that. I respect that.

I never seen that before. I never seen a thing be sick but it was nothing…like minus sick…negative sick. You can come out now baby and we can go over to mine and we'll both wear the watch today, ok baby. Yeah?

YOU TALKING TO ME?

I've lived with Robert now…for about …three months. Going quite well…sorry, De Niro that is, obviously. Robert De Niro to use his full name. I assume some of you will have heard of him…um… perhaps some of you haven't I dunno. If you haven't… um…not quite sure what's happened there. Don't know what universe you've been inhabiting. He's pretty famous – just go and rent one of his DVDs, you know, any of them – massive body of work. So we met…or just join Love Film, you know the online film-rental service. There's lots of his films on there. It's incredibly easy to join. I'm on the 2 DVDs a month for £2.99 deal. Which is just about right for me, you may require more films than that, or less…although I think that's the minimum…2 a month.

Now, *(Starts laughing.)* sorry I'm just remembering… it's such a funny story *(Laughs some more.)* how we met…so funny! So I'm working in this toy shop in Sudbury, when who should come in through the door but, you've guessed it…Bobby De Niro. He says he's looking for a toy guitar for his nephew. So, I'm showing him all our musical instruments for years 5 and upwards and we're chatting away, you know and I say, Robert I think you're an astonishing actor you know…what are you doing in Sudbury? He says, well mainly buying a toy guitar and we both laugh. And then I say, no but seriously Robert, you're such an astonishing actor, but I was wandering if you've ever thought of doing any Shakespeare?

And he goes, and I'm going to do the accent now, so you'll have to excuse me, he says, 'I've always thought my neck was too short for Shakespeare'.

Which was a slightly odd answer, so then I respond with,

'But Robert, does the packaging always match the product? This plastic toy guitar here says on the box that it'll make you the greatest guitar player ever…but you don't actually believe it do you. It's what's inside the box that matters.

'You're neck may have thickened but, My God you're still an astonishing actor, who could play any part they liked. And with that he asked me out for shellfish.

Her phone goes off.

Oh sorry that's me…*(Gets it out of pocket and looks.)* It's Robert.

Hi Robert, I was just saying that…what?

As exiting.

…well of course I'm talking to you. Yes, I'm talking to you. Well who else would I be talking to…there's no one else here…yes I'm talking to you…